What Shall We Do Today?

By the same author:
Fingers Feet and Fun!

What Shall We Do Today?

*Stories, rhymes
and things to make*

DELPHINE EVANS
Illustrated by Sheila Carter

Hutchinson

London Melbourne Sydney Auckland Johannesburg

Hutchinson Children's Books Ltd
An imprint of the Hutchinson Publishing Group
17–21 Conway Street, London W1P 6JD

Hutchinson Publishing Group (Australia) Pty Ltd
16–22 Church Street, Hawthorn, Melbourne, Victoria 3122, Australia

Hutchinson Group (NZ) Ltd
32–34 View Road, PO Box 40-086, Glenfield, Auckland 10

Hutchinson Group (SA) Pty Ltd
PO Box 337, Bergvlei 2012, South Africa

First published 1985

© Delphine Evans 1985
Illustrations © Sheila Carter 1985

Set in Plantin by Book Ens, Saffron Walden, Essex

Printed and bound in Great Britain by Anchor Brendon Ltd, Tiptree, Essex

British Library Cataloguing in Publication Data
Evans, Delphine
What shall we do today?
1. Amusements
I. Title   II. Carter, Sheila
649'.5   GV1203

ISBN 0 09 160400 1

Contents

Introduction   9

Weather Day   11
The North Wind   *Story*   11
Wind   *Follow up rhyme*   13
What am I?   *Weather riddles*   14
Storm Cat   *Noise story*   15
Weather Clock   *Something to make*   16
Wind and Rain   *Rhymes for fun*   18

Animal Day   19
Tale of an Elephant's
  Tail   *Story*   19
I am a Dragon   *Action rhyme*   21
Can You Guess?   *Animal riddles*   22
Mr Squirrel   *Rhyme*   23
Donkey Finger
  Puppet   *Something to make*   24
Anna's Day   *Noise story*   26

Bird Day   28
The Greedy Robin   *Story*   28
If   *Action rhyme*   31
The Wren   *Rhyme*   32
Robin   *Rhyme*   33
Bird Finger Puppet   *Something to make*   34
Birds   *Rhymes for fun*   36

Nature Day 37

A Present from Grandad	Story	37
I'm a Pretty Flower	Action rhyme	41
Growing	Flower riddles	42
Autumn Leaves	Rhyme	43
My Fish	Rhyme	43
Fish in a Jar	Something to make	44
My Snail	Rhyme	45
Butterfly Finger Puppet and Mobile	Things to make	46
Conkers	Rhyme	49

Colours Day 50

Roy the Hat Boy	Story	50
Peter's Magic Paint	Rhyme for finger painting	53
Colour Counting	Finger game	54
Do You Know?	Colour riddles	55
'Talk About Colour' Book	Something to make	56
All Change!	Colour game	57

Numbers, Words and Letters Day 58

Do Not Touch	Story	58
Ten Big Giants	Action song	61
What Shall We Do?	Action rhyme	62
Sounds Like . . .	Guessing game	63
Things to Eat and Drink	Food alphabet	64
Number One	Finger rhyme	65

Town Day 66

Trumper's Trip to Town	*Story*	66
Crossing the Street	*Traffic action rhyme*	70
I Spy	*Town riddles*	71
Bookworm	*Something to make*	72
Emma Goes Shopping	*Noise story*	73

Home Day 75

Gran's New Home	*Story*	75
Katy Kitten	*Action rhyme*	78
In My House	*Home riddles*	79
My House	*Something to make*	80
Mrs Cat's Cake	*Story rhyme*	82
What Shall I Wear Today?	*Rhyme*	83
Look Around	*Safety rhyme*	83
Early in the Morning	*Listening rhyme*	84

Seaside Day 85

Roy the Hat Boy Goes to the Seaside	*Story*	85
Pretend	*Action rhyme*	88
Octopus	*Something to make*	89
Waves and Pebbles	*Rhymes for fun*	90
The a, b and sea	*Seaside alphabet*	92

Easter Days   93

The Moonstruck
  Chicken   *Story*   93
Church Bells   *Action rhyme*   95
What Am I?   *Easter riddles*   96
Easter Basket   *Something to make*   97
Easter Tree   *Something to make*   98
Eggshell Humpty   *Something to make*   100

Christmas Days   101

The Wundawot   *Story*   101
Father Christmas   *Noise Story*   104
Christmas Bells   *Something to make*   106
Baby Jesus   *Rhyme*   107
Santa in a Chimney   *Something to make*   108
X is for Xmas   *Christmas*
                alphabet 110

INTRODUCTION

When my children were young, there were many times when I needed help. Especially when I required instant ideas which would interest and amuse them and would at the same time have some educational value.

Working with groups of children, I found this need again, whenever I wanted to co-ordinate a theme idea into a project. For example, if I decided to use weather, I needed to find a story, an action rhyme, a game, something to make and do, which linked together. So first I had to hunt for a suitable story, then an action rhyme and so on. By the time I had found these in different places, my enthusiasm had begun to wane.

Travelling around, I talked to groups of people and found they had exactly the same problems.

This book will solve them all for you.

Each chapter follows a theme through, with stories, rhymes, things to make and do, riddles and games – all on the same subject.

It can be used in many ways – in the home or in groups.

As a whole day project.

As a morning or afternoon project.

For Storytimes – using one or two ideas.

As an activity book.

At parties – using the noise stories, riddles and games.

As a guide to get you started on a project, adding your own ideas as you progress.

As with *Fingers, Feet and Fun!*, the contents have all been tried and found to be successful, which has shown me once again that learning CAN be fun.

I hope you will agree.

Delphine Evans

Weather Day

The North Wind

No one liked the North Wind. He always came in
Winter and he always made people cold.

Whenever he was around everyone wore hats,
gloves and scarves.

'Brr . . . isn't it cold?' they said.

The birds all tried to find shelter, the flowers
hid beneath their leaves and all the doors and
windows were closed tightly – so that he couldn't
find a way in.

Sometimes – just sometimes – he made the
children happy, if he could find some snow to
bring with him. This winter he had not found one
flake, so he'd blown around on his own.

Whirling and twirling, in all the corners he
could find. Blowing, freezing everything and every-
body.

'I wish this North Wind would go,' people said,
and they pulled up their collars and hurried out of
his way.

'I'll go and find some snow – at least the
children will like me then,' he said and blew back
to the North Pole. But, when he arrived at the
Pole, the snow had already left.

11

'I won't be welcome for a long time,' he thought, and tucked himself into a cloud and fell fast asleep.

Some time later, he awoke, yawned, stretched and thought, 'I'll have one quick gust before the Winter ends.'

He was over the sea when he first started to feel funny. The air around him seemed to be warm. By the time he reached land, he was feeling very hot. He looked up. There was the sun, shining brightly above him.

'What's the matter with you,' said the wind to the sun. 'You're not usually so hot.'

'Oh yes I am,' replied the sun, 'in the Summer.'

'Summer?'

'Yes. I can't understand why you're around. North Winds are supposed to blow in winter – not Summer.'

'Good gracious, I DID oversleep, but since I'm here I'll have a quick flip around, just to see what things look like in the Summer,' said the wind.

How different everything looked. There were leaves on all the trees, the grass was long and green, flowers were everywhere and the birds were singing.

Windows and doors were wide open and the people had no gloves or scarves on. Their arms and legs were bare and they were lying around all over the place – in parks and gardens, beside rivers and the sea.

Everywhere the wind went they all said: 'What a lovely breeze.' They liked him and wanted him to stay.

'I'd like to stay, really I would,' he puffed. 'But I'm so hot. I'll have to go.'

Before he did, there was one thing he had to do. He had always wanted to go inside a house. In the winter when all the doors and windows were closed, it was impossible – although he often tried. So, in he blew, through the door and from one room to another. He was surprised how hot and stuffy it was inside.

'I'm off home,' he said and blew out through a window. The curtains folded around him and made him hotter than ever. 'The summer is no time for me, even if people are pleased to see me.'

And off he went back to the North Pole – to sleep until Winter.

Wind

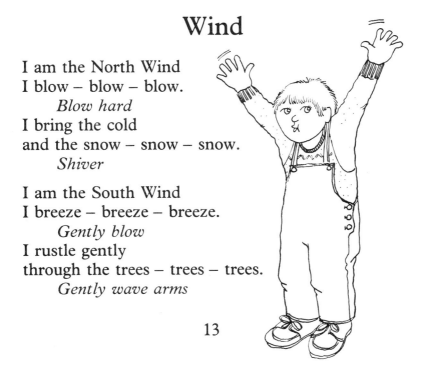

I am the North Wind
I blow – blow – blow.
   Blow hard
I bring the cold
and the snow – snow – snow.
   Shiver

I am the South Wind
I breeze – breeze – breeze.
   Gently blow
I rustle gently
through the trees – trees – trees.
   Gently wave arms

13

What Am I?

1   I make you wet,
        If you're out in the town.
    I never go up –
        I always come down!

    Answer: Rain.

2   I come from the south
        And the east and the west.
    But if I'm from the north
        Then do wear a vest!

    Answer: Wind.

3   I come in the winter
        Falling quiet and white.
    Sometimes by day
        And sometimes by night!

    Answer: Snow.

4   I make a loud noise
        High up in the sky.
    I rumble and tumble
        As I roll by!

    Answer: Thunder.

5   I'm yellow and hot
        You like me a lot!

    Answer: Sun.

14

Storm Cat

Miaeow!

This is great fun. The storyteller reads the story and pauses where indicated by —— for the children/ child to make the sounds.

It can be extra funny if a cassette or tape recorder is used. Turn it on to record at the start and then play back – you'll be surprised at the results!

Today is cold and windy —— and Marmaduke the cat —— is lost in the woods. It's beginning to rain —— and he can hear thunder ——.

The little stream ✕ had turned into a raging torrent ——. Marmaduke climbed into a tree, right to the top, and couldn't get down.

He wished he could be rescued, and thought, 'I need a fire engine —— with a long ladder. It's raining —— and thundering —— and the little

15

stream —✕— has changed into a raging torrent. ——'
and he cried ——.

Like magic a fire engine —— arrived, driven by
Mr Gunn —✕—. 'How did you get up there, little
cat? It's very windy —— but hold tight, we'll soon
rescue you.'

Mr Gunn —✕— climbed the ladder, right to the
top of the creaky tree —✕— and rescued Marmaduke
the cat ——. It was still raining —— and thundering —— and the little stream —✕— was still a
raging torrent ——. Marmaduke purred —✕—. He
was so happy to have been rescued.

who was a very happy man.

Listen very carefully

Make a Weather Clock

What you need

Paper plate
Small length of cardboard
Glue
Felt tips
Paper fastener like the one in the picture

What you do

1   Divide your paper plate into four parts.
2   Draw a picture in each of the parts, to show
    different kinds of weather: rain, sun, cloud,
    snow.

16

3 Cut a pointer from cardboard.
4 Colour it with your felt tips, and secure to centre of your weather clock with the paper fastener.
5 Point it towards today's weather.

Note: You can divide your clock into as many weather parts as you like and include wind, showers, fog, etc.

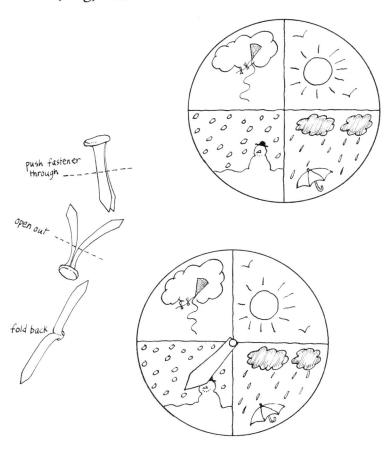

Wind and Rain

Hear the wind,
  See the wind, blowing things about.
See a man
  Lose his hat – hear him give a shout.

Oh how I love a rainy day,
  If I can go outside and play.
I wear a bright red mackintosh,
  And boots that let me splish and splosh!

The sun is nice and keeps me hot,
  And wind is fun – it blows a lot.
But most of all I like to dash,
  Through puddles going splish and splash!

Down comes the rain,
  Down comes the rain,
Up goes my umbrella again.
  Red ones, green ones,
All over town,
  Up they go – when the rain comes down.

The doors open wide,
  Walk outside.
Pitter, patter, see the rain –
  Quickly, back inside again.

Animal Day

Tale of an Elephant's Tail

Have you ever wondered why an enormous animal like the elephant has a long trunk, but a tiny tail?

Many, many years ago, a severe storm raged throughout the world. The animals didn't mind the thunder, or the lightning, or the rain. It was the wind that frightened them. They had never before known a wind blow so hard or so long.

The storm continued for five days, but at last it was over. The animals were delighted – until they looked at each other. It was no wonder they had all felt peculiar during the storm. The wind had blown their tails off! Not one could be seen anywhere.

A meeting was called to decide what should be done.

'I propose we make up a search party,' said the lion.

'We shall want more than one,' said the tiger.

Everyone started to talk at the same time. During the commotion, an eagle flew down and landed on a stone – right in the middle of the group.

'I think I can guess what all this noise is about,' he said. 'You've lost your tails!'

19

'Yes, yes, that's right,' shouted the lion. 'Can you help us?'

'As a matter of fact, I can. I know exactly where they are.'

Suddenly it was very quiet and everyone waited for the eagle to continue.

'About five kilometres to the east I saw an enormous mountain that I did not recognize. When I flew down to have a look at it, I was amazed. It was a mountain of tails.'

The animals didn't wait to hear any more. They were off as fast as they could go to look for the mountain.

The jaguar and the tiger reached it first and started sorting through the huge pile of tails. The tiger soon recognized his striped tail and the jaguar his spotted one. They laid the tails on the ground and sat down – very hard. When they stood up again their tails were firmly attached once more.

By this time there were quite a lot more animals searching through the pile and tails were scattered everywhere. The monkey found his quite easily because it was so long and curly. The black panther soon found his and so did the lion – he recognized the little tassel on the end.

The elephant travelled much more slowly than the others and, when at last he arrived, there were only two tails left – one very large and one very small. He walked up to the large one and was having a look at it when he slipped and fell head first on top of it. When he stood up again, the large tail was attached firmly – to his nose! He shook his head, trying hard to get rid of it, overbalanced, and sat down firmly – on the little tail.

When he eventually managed to get back on his feet again there stood the elephant – with a large tail at the front and a small tail at the back!

That's how he's been ever since.

I am a Dragon

I am a dragon – fierce and strong.
   Stand straight, looking fierce.
I have flip flop wings and a tail SO long.
   Wave arms and indicate long tail.
My wings go flip, flop, just like this.
   Continue waving arms.
And my tail goes swish, swish, swish, swish, swish.
   Move 'tail' end side to side.

I'm not really a dragon that goes flip, flop, swish.
   Indicate wings and tail.
Because I'm ME – but I wish, wish, wish.
That I WAS a dragon, fierce and strong.
   Stand straight – looking fierce.
With flip flop wings and a tail SO long!
   Indicate wings and tail.

Can You Guess?

1   If you'd like to play a game,
Can you guess this animal's name?
In the country he can be found,
He looks like a ball when he's curled up round.
See him move – there's a long pointed nose,
And tiny claws on the end of his toes.
His prickly spikes are short and straight.
In winter time, he will hibernate!

Answer: Hedgehog

2   Two little legs and two webbed feet,
Two little wings and a beak to eat.
Swimming on the water, waiting to be fed,
He dives underneath and you can't see his head.
Out of the water, waddling around,
Always making a quacking sound!

Answer: Duck

3   A cow has one that is swishy.
A squirrel has one that is bushy.
A pig has one that is curly.
A cat has one that is twirly.
A cockerel has one that stands up tall.
But a guinea pig hasn't got one at all!

Answer: Tail

4   A dog has four and so has a cat
     A chicken has two – did you guess that?
     A table has them and so has a chair.
     A tiger has four and so has a bear.
     A centipede has lots to help him crawl,
     But a worm and a snake have none at all!

Answer: Legs

Mr Squirrel

Mr Squirrel, bushy tail,
  Busy as can be.
See him gather nuts to keep
  For his winter tea.
Up and down the tree he goes –
  In and out his nest.
Finding all the hazel nuts
  That he likes the best.
Soon he has brought in enough
  For his winter store.
Tired little squirrel
  Goes inside and shuts the door.

Make a
Donkey Finger Puppet

What you need

A piece of felt, foam or fur approximately 10 cm ×
    10 cm
Oddments of wool and felt
Tracing paper and ordinary paper 10 cm × 10 cm
Glue

What you do

1   Trace the donkey shape on to paper and cut
    out. This is your pattern.

24

2 Pin your pattern to the material and cut round it. You now have a donkey shape in material.
3 Make eyes, nose and a bridle from the felt and wool oddments. Glue in place (as shown).
4 If you are not using fur for the face, make a furry or wool mane.
5 Glue the dotted lines together and your donkey finger puppet is ready to use.

Things to do

1 Think of a name for him.
2 Put him on your middle finger. Your thumb and other fingers will be his legs.
3 Practise making his head nod.

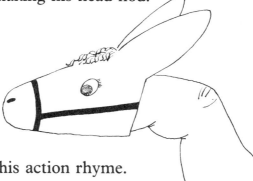

4 Now try this action rhyme.

Two little eyes with which to see,
   Point out eyes.
Two little ears to listen to me,
   Point out ears.
One little nose and a soft mane too,
   Touch nose and mane.
One little mouth saying 'How do you do!'
   Nod his head.

Anna's Day

This is great fun. The storyteller reads the story and pauses where indicated by —— for the children/child to make the sounds.

It can be extra funny if a cassette or tape recorder is used. Turn it to record at the start and then play back – you'll be surprised at the results.

You can practise one or two noises before you start.

Anna was excited, as the train —— travelled out of the town ——. She was going to the country to stay with Farmer Stamp ——.

At the gate she saw a gaggle of white, long-necked geese ——.

'Look here,' said Farmer Stamp ——. 'Here's a flock of sheep ——, wool is made from their fleece.'

Then Anna saw a herd of cows —— in a meadow. Flowing through the meadow was a rippling stream —— and she spotted a shoal of tiny fish swimming.

Back in the farmyard, Farmer Stamp —— showed her a litter of puppies —— belonging to Lass the sheepdog ——.

In the chicken —— run was a brood of chicks —— only two days old. Mother Hen scratched about —— looking for things to eat —— and the cockerel —— strutted about, crowing.

Later that evening, when they had finished tea ——, Anna saw a pride of lions —— on Farmer Stamp's —— television.

Just before going to bed, Mrs Stamp —— gave Anna a glass of fresh milk to drink ——.

Anna fell asleep listening to the hooting of a barn owl ——.

Bird Day

The Greedy Robin

In the garden of 2 West Street was a bird table.
The family who lived there always made sure it
was filled with plenty to eat and drink.

At first there had been many birds in the
garden, but now there was only one – a greedy,
bad-tempered, selfish robin. He made sure no
other birds came into his territory and, even when
he couldn't manage to eat all the food himself, he
would never share it.

One winter's day, he was waiting for the titbits.
As he hopped up and down he said to himself,
'There will be lovely bacon rind and cake crumbs,

fat from the meat, nuts and something nice to
drink.'

A long time later he was still waiting. He jumped
on the window sill and looked inside. There
seemed to be no one around.

It was getting dark now, and there were no
cheerful lights in the house.

Poor robin was beginning to feel very hungry
and cold. Flakes of snow were starting to fall, so
he flew to a sheltered perch in the branches of his
fir tree and tried to sleep. All night long he kept
dreaming of food.

When at last it was morning, he flew straight to
the bird table. It was covered with snow. No one
had brushed it off and no one had put out anything to eat or drink.

He flew to the wall which separated the garden
from next door and watched the other birds
happily feeding and drinking fresh water.

A sparrow saw him and asked what the trouble
was.

'I'm hungry,' said the robin.

'We've often been hungry,' replied the sparrow.
'But you wouldn't share anything with us.'

'I know,' answered the robin. 'I never realized
until now how horrible it felt to be hungry.'

The sparrow didn't feel a bit sorry for him. In
fact he thought it was about time someone taught
him a lesson.

'Your family have gone away for a holiday,' he
told the robin. 'They must have forgotten about
the bird table. They won't be back for days and

days,' and he flew off to chew another piece of bacon rind.

Robin stayed on the wall and watched, hoping that perhaps a little of something would come his way – but it didn't.

Night came again and there were still no lights in the house. It was even worse trying to sleep that night and he was extremely glad when morning came.

He flew straight to the bird table – but it was still empty.

By this time he was beginning to feel quite ill and the birds next door started to feel sorry for him.

'I think he has learned his lesson now,' said the sparrow. 'Let's invite him across.'

Robin was delighted and promised them he would never be greedy again.

I wonder if he kept his promise.

'If'

If I was a bird, I'd sing and fly,
 Stand still and flap arms.
Flying fast and flying high,
 Run around on tiptoe and make bird noises.
Flying slow,
 Slow down.
Flying low.
 Lower arms and body.
I'd land on a stone and look around,
 Pretend to land and look around.
To see what insects could be found.
 Continue looking.
I spy a cat
Big and fat.
 Pretend to see cat.
Flying fast and flying high,
 Jump up and fly.
Back again into the sky.

31

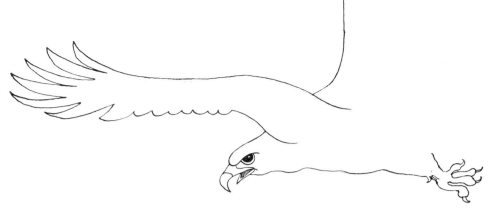

The Wren

The tiny brown wren is the king of all the birds,
  they say.
Do you know the story of how this happened one
  day?
It was declared, the bird who could fly the highest
  would be king,
No matter what the body size, or shape, or length
  of wing.
The eagle said, 'There is no doubt, of course it will
  be me.'
The smaller birds looked at each other and
  whispered, 'We shall see.'

Many tried and then at last it was the eagle's turn.
The little brown wren, although so small, was very
  quick to learn.
He hid beneath the eagle's wing and stayed there
  all the time.

The eagle soon became quite tired – the little wren
　　felt fine.
And when the eagle thought he'd won, the wren
　　flew from his wing.
And up and up and up he went, which made the
　　wren – the KING!

Robin

I can see a robin,
Hop, hop, hop.
Please, little robin,
Stop, stop, stop.

You have feathers,
Some red – some brown.
Please say 'hello'
As you hop around.

Where are your ears?
I'd like to know.
Where do you hide
In the winter snow?

You wave your wings,
And off you fly.
Over the trees,
And into the sky.

Please, little robin,
Say 'hello'.
Tell me things
I want to know.

Make a
Bird Finger Puppet

What you need

Glue
Felt tips or crayons or paints
Scissors
Tracing paper
Sheet of plain paper

What you do

1 Trace the two pattern pieces from this page, and transfer your tracing to plain paper.
2 Colour and cut out.
3 Glue the two dotted lines of the body together, to make a tube for your finger. Glue the body tube to the wings. Your bird puppet is now ready to fly.

Things to do

Put your puppet on your finger and use it with this rhyme.

See my bird – watch him fly,
  Make him fly about like a bird.
Sometimes low, sometimes high,
  Make him fly high and low.
Straight and fast or up and down,
  Do as the actions suggest.
Sometimes circling round and round.
  Do as the actions suggest.

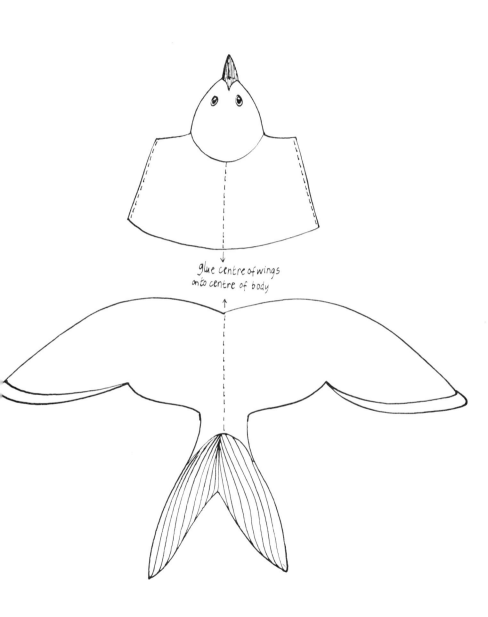

glue centre of wings
onto centre of body

Birds

Listen

Listen to the birds singing a song,
  Sometimes short, sometimes long.
Tweet-tweet-tweet they seem to say,
  Singing to us all through the day.

Blackbird

A blackbird is black from his head to his wings.
  He sits in a bush and he sings and he sings.
He opens his beak, which is brilliant yellow,
  To tell us all he's a happy fellow.

Cuckoo

The cuckoo is a funny bird,
  Rarely seen, but often heard.
Never builds herself a nest,
  But uses those of all the rest!

Nature Day

A Present from Grandad

Simon loved to see his grandfather and looked forward to his visits. He always brought him something special, not sweets and toys like other people brought, but exciting, interesting things. Simon could see him coming up the path and ran to meet him.

'Hello, Simon. How's my big boy today?' Grandad asked. Simon liked it when he called him 'big boy'.

'I'm fine, thank you, Grandad,' he replied. He was longing to know what his grandfather had brought and was jumping up and down with excitement.

'Can you guess what I've found for you today?' asked Grandad. Simon thought a little and said:

'Give me a clue.'

'It's small and it's black.'

'Is it a piece of coal?' asked Simon.

'No,' replied Grandad. 'It moves – but it has no legs.'

Simon thought for a long while and wondered how anything could move if it didn't have legs. Then he had an idea.

'Does it fly?' he asked.

'No.'

'Oh dear,' replied Simon, and thought some more. 'Has it feathers or fur?'

'Neither,' replied Grandad.

Simon really was stuck now. It must be something very peculiar that Grandad had brought this time. How could it move without walking or flying? And if it didn't have feathers or fur – then it must wear clothes.

So, very slowly, he asked. 'Does it wear clothes?'

Once again the answer was 'No.'

'I give up,' said Simon.

'I'll tell you what,' said Grandad. 'I'll give you another big clue. It lives under water.'

'It swims. It swims, that's how it moves,' said Simon. 'It's a fish!'

'Yes, it swims,' replied Grandad. 'But it's not a fish.'

'Then I don't know what it is,' said Simon. 'Please tell me.'

'It's a *tadpole* – in fact it's two tadpoles,' Grandad told him, and showed him a glass jar full of water, with two funny little black things swimming around, wriggling their tails.

Simon looked through the glass and said 'TADPOLE', very slowly. It was a word he had not heard before. Then he said, 'But you told me it wasn't a fish and it is.'

'It looks very like a fish at the moment,' Grandad replied, 'but tadpoles are really baby frogs.'

Although Simon had never seen a tadpole, he had seen a frog. These small black shiny creatures didn't look like baby frogs at all.

'Frogs have legs and they jump about and they're green and they don't have tails,' he said all at once.

'You're a clever boy to think of that,' Grandad answered. 'That's why this present is so interesting. You can watch these tadpoles grow and change into frogs.' He placed the jar on a window sill where Simon could watch them.

Every morning when he got up, the first thing Simon did was to look at his tadpoles. Gradually their bodies became larger and their tails smaller and the water dirtier.

Grandad often changed the dirty water for clean and planted fresh weeds in the stones on the bottom, for the tadpoles to nibble.

It was fun watching them change shape and one day, to his great delight, Simon saw that two tiny legs had begun to grow. As the first two legs became longer, two more appeared, and it was then that Grandad brought a small piece of wood and floated it on the water.

'You'll soon be needing this,' he told Simon. 'When your tadpoles are frogs, they'll want to come out of the water to breathe.'

Simon had waited so long he thought they would always be tadpoles. Then, one morning when he looked into the jar, it was empty. He looked at the piece of wood and there sitting on it were two tiny green frogs!

39

That day when Grandad arrived Simon was extremely excited, but he calmed down a little when Grandad explained to him that he couldn't keep frogs in a jar.

'I'll tell you what,' Grandad said. 'We'll take them to the pond in the park.'

When they reached the pond Grandad placed the jar on the soft grass. They kept very quiet and the two tiny frogs hopped out of the jar and on to a large stone. Then they jumped off again and wriggled underneath.

Simon laughed, because he knew that his frogs would be happier outdoors. Then he stopped, for there was something puzzling him.

'What's happened to my tadpoles' tails?' he asked.

Do you know what happened to their tails? See if you can find out.

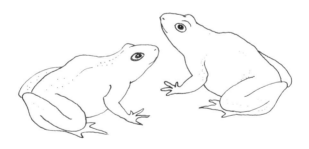

I'm a Pretty Flower

I'm a pretty flower,
Stand straight, hands by sides.
Swaying in the breeze.
Sway.
My legs are my stem,
My hands are my leaves.
Keeping hands still, lift palms.
Along came a butterfly
And landed on my nose.
Wriggle nose.
Along came a rabbit
And sat upon my toes.
Wriggle toes.
I moved my head a little
Move head.
And the butterfly flew away.
Then the baby rabbit
Ran away to play.
Wriggle toes again.
So now I'm just a flower,
Swaying in the breeze.
Sway.
My legs are my stem,
My hands are my leaves.
Sway with hands as leaves, as before.

Growing

Growing in the springtime
A flower can be seen.
Its head is yellow
Its stem is green.
A trumpet top
And leaves smooth and long.
Swaying in the breeze,
So delicate, yet strong.

Answer: Daffodil

Growing in the lawn
A flower can be seen.
Small and white and yellow,
It makes a pretty scene.
If it's cut – it grows again,
It's sometimes used
To make a chain.

Answer: Daisy

Growing in the flower-bed
Flowers can be seen.
Lots of coloured heads
With small leaves in between.
Purple, blue and yellow
Looking towards the sun,
They seem like pretty faces
Smiling at everyone.

Answer: Pansies

Autumn Leaves

The trees are standing tall and bare
  In winter they've no clothes to wear.
No leaves on the ash or the old oak tree,
  They're on the ground, for us all to see,
Piled in layers around the roots.
  Making nice warm winter boots!

My Fish

I looked at my fish in the morning,
I looked at my fish at night.
Then I noticed something
That didn't seem quite right.
His eyes were always open.
It puzzled me a lot.
I wondered if he ever slept
Or if he just forgot.
I suppose he must get tired
Swimming round all day.
If my fish could tell me,
I wonder what he'd say.

Make Fish in a Jar

What you need

Kitchen foil
Cotton
Pencil
Glass jar

What you do

1   Cut fish shapes from kitchen foil.
2   Thread them on some cotton and tie the cotton round the middle of your pencil.

3   Balance the pencil across the top of the jar with the fish hanging inside.

My Snail

Once I found a snail
  On a winter's day.
I turned him all around
  But he didn't want to play.
I found a door so thick
  I really couldn't tell
If he was inside
  Hiding in his shell.
I put him carefully back
  In a hole in the wall.
When springtime came around
  He wasn't there at all.
At first I could not find him,
  Then I saw his silver trail,
Up and down and over stones,
  There I found my snail.
Out of his shell he poked his head
  To show his tiny eye,
Right on the end of a wriggly horn
  Looking at passers-by.
Slowly the other horn came out
  Moving round and round.
'Hello,' I said – but the snail popped in
  And never made a sound.

Make a Butterfly Finger Puppet and Mobile

Finger puppet

What you need

Glue
Felt tips *or* crayons *or* paints
Scissors
Tracing paper
Sheet of white paper

What you do

1　Trace both these illustrations (A and B) and transfer your tracing to plain white paper.
2　Colour and cut out.
3　Glue the two dotted lines along the edge of piece B together to make a tube for your finger.
4　Glue centre of A to centre of B.
5　Paint a face on your finger before you put it inside your puppet.

Things to do

Put the puppet on your finger, make it fly about and say this rhyme.

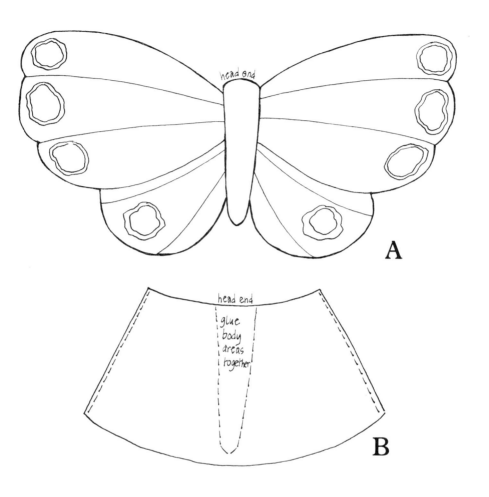

A

head end

B

head end
glue
body
areas
together

A butterfly flutters quietly,
   Makes no noise at all.
A butterfly flutters quietly,
   Does it have a call?
Listen very carefully
   As it passes by.
See it flutter gently –
   And away into the sky.

Mobile

What you need

Coloured or white paper
Glue
Felt tips, crayons or paints
Strong cord
Scissors
2 pieces of dowel or strong cardboard 30 cm long

What you do

1   Trace the butterfly's wings from this illustration.

2   Transfer your tracing to white or coloured
    paper – make five copies.
3   Colour and cut out.
4   Cut the cord into five pieces and knot one end
    of each. Thread through centre of each butterfly.

48

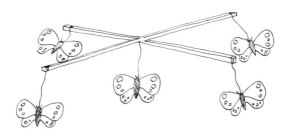

5 Glue dowel or cardboard in centre to make a cross. Tie a butterfly on to each corner and one in the centre.

6 Cut a long piece of cord and tie around centre of cross. Hang up and watch your butterfly mobile move.

Conkers

Chestnut tree, growing tall,
  Standing on a hill.
Find a conker, string it up
  And keep it very still.
See it dangle on its string,
  A round shiny ball.
Ready, steady, direct hit –
  Nothing left at all!

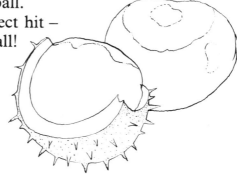

Colours Day

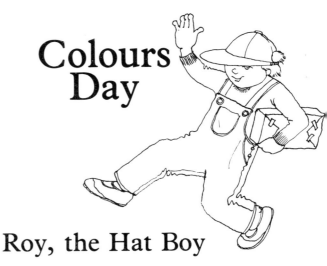

Roy, the Hat Boy

Note to storyteller: The rhyme about Roy and his hat is repeated several times, and it is fun for the children/child to join in each time it is repeated.

Roy loved wearing hats. In fact, it was most unusual to see him without one. Whenever people saw him they said, 'Here comes Roy – and his hat.' And when they saw the hat he was wearing, 'Well I never – fancy that!'

Today Roy was feeling sad. He had been invited to a Yellow Party that afternoon, and this meant you had to wear as many yellow things as you could.

He had a yellow jumper and yellow socks and he wanted his yellow hat too – but he couldn't find it anywhere.

There was a knock on the door and his friend Sam asked, 'Would you like to come to the park with Mum and me?'

'No, thank you,' replied Roy.

'Why not,' asked Sam.

'I've lost my yellow hat.'

'Well, you've plenty of others,' replied Sam.

'But I want my yellow one for the party.'

His mother suggested that he went to the park whilst she had a really good look for his hat.

'Oh, all right, but I must find a hat to wear,' said Roy, and he went off to his hat box.

He chose a black peaked one – then he could pretend he was in charge of the park. When he walked back into the room they all said,

'Here comes Roy – and his hat.

Well I never – fancy that!'

He usually smiled back. But not today.

On their way to the park they passed quite a few other friends who all said,

'Here comes Roy – and his hat.

Well I never – fancy that!'

There were still no smiles from Roy – he was thinking about his yellow hat. It was one of his favourites; when he was wearing it, he felt very important. It was a digger driver's hat. His dad had been given it by a real digger driver and Roy wore it as often as he could.

When they reached the park, the man in charge looked at him and said,

'Here comes Roy – and his hat.

Well I never – fancy that!'

Roy was still unhappy. But then Sam's mum took out the football and for a while he forgot about his hat. He loved playing football with Sam

51

and they ran and ran until they were both exhausted.

'Come on, you two,' called Sam's mum. 'Time to go home.'

'Just two more minutes,' said Sam, but Roy was ready to go when he'd been reminded of home.

'I wonder if Mum's found my yellow hat?'

On the way back, the butcher came out of his shop to say good morning to Sam and his mum – but to Roy he said,

'Here comes Roy – and his hat.

Well I never – fancy that!'

Roy managed a small smile this time, because he had a feeling his mother would have found his hat.

As soon as he arrived home he asked her, 'Have you found my yellow hat?'

'I'm sorry, Roy,' she answered. 'I've hunted everywhere. I can't think what has happened to it.'

He almost cried then, but stopped when he heard a knock on the door and a voice call, 'Where's Roy, the Hat Boy?'

Roy recognized the barber's voice. He liked the barber because only yesterday when he'd finished cutting his hair he'd given him a new hat. It was made of cardboard with writing all over it.

He went to the door and the barber was holding the lost yellow hat.

'I think this must be yours. You were so eager to wear my hat home, you forgot this one.'

Roy jumped up and down with delight. He hugged his yellow hat to him and grinned at the barber.

'Thank you, thank you,' he said over and over
again.

He went to the party that afternoon wearing his
yellow socks and jumper *and* his yellow hat. When
he walked in they all said,

'Here comes Roy – and his hat.

Well I never – fancy that!'

and Roy smiled an enormous smile!

Peter's Magic Paint

Peter felt like painting, but a brush he could not
  find.

So he used his finger – he hoped no one would
  mind.

He dipped it into yellow and then into the red.

He put it on some paper and round and round it
  spread.

But, to his surprise – it was ORANGE he could
  see.

Yellow and red had disappeared. Wherever could
  they be?

*You can do some finger painting like Peter. Try it
and see if you can find where the red and yellow go.*

Colour Counting

Starting with the thumb, stick a coloured paper circle on each nail: Red – blue – yellow – white and green.

Begin with the hand held up, palm away from your face. As you say the rhyme, bend your finger away from you to make it disappear.

Red – blue – yellow – white and green,
Wriggle each one as you say its colour.
The funniest fingers you have ever seen.
Wriggle them all.
1 – 2 – 3 – 4 – 5.
All my fingers are alive!
Continue wriggling.
But, Mr Red –
went to bed.
Bend 'red' finger.
Now I've only four.
Mr Blue –
went there too.
Bend 'blue' finger.
Now I've only three.
Mr Yellow –
said 'Hello'.
Bend 'yellow' finger.
Now I've only two.
Mr White –
had a fright.
Bend 'white' finger.

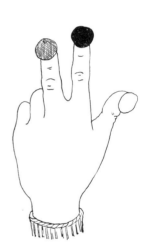

Now I've only one.
Mr Green –
          couldn't be seen.
     Bend green finger.
Now – there's – none – at – all!

Do You Know?

A glass of milk,
Teeth that are bright
Do you know the colour?
It is ...
White.

A great big elephant
And a little mouse will play.
Do you know their colour?
It is ...
Grey.

Leaves on the flowers
And grass can be seen.
Do you know this colour?
It is ...
Green.

Bluebells in the woods
The sea and sky too
Can you guess this colour?
It is ...
Blue.

Make a
'Talk About Colour' Book

What you need

As many different plain coloured pieces of material as possible, including 'see through' ones of blue, yellow and red.

What you do

1   Using pinking shears cut the material into 'pages' 10 cm × 15 cm.
2   Join all together (glue, sew or staple) along one of the short edges, making sure the flimsy ones are placed blue – yellow – red. Your book is now ready to use.

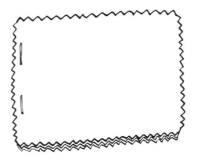

The 'Talkabout Book' will start the child/children talking about colours.

The 'see through' pages can be used to indicate how colours can be mixed: blue and yellow shown together make green; yellow and red will make orange.

All Change!

This game can be played with children in groups. It is an easy game for young children at parties – and they are learning about colours at the same time.

How to play – easy way

1   Children stand in a circle.
2   Adult calls a colour, e.g. 'Red'.
3   All the children wearing that colour go to the middle of the circle.
4   Adult calls 'All change', and children return to circle.
5   Then another colour is called – 'Green', etc. . . .

How to play – harder way

Instead of calling a colour only, call an article of clothing or part of the body.
e.g. 'Brown shoes.'
    'All change.'
  'Blue eyes.'
    'All change.'
  'Red tops.'
    'All change.'
  'White socks.'

Numbers, Words and Letters Day

Do Not Touch

Note to storyteller: As an aid to this story make a sign with the words 'Do Not Touch' on it. Use it whenever it is mentioned in the story and maybe your child/children will learn to 'read' it just like Nick.

No one except his mother ever called Nicholas by his proper name. Most of his friends called him Nick, and sometimes he was called Naughty Nick! Quite often he didn't even know he was being naughty. Only that morning when he had been

58

shopping with his mum, she had grumbled at him.

They were in the greengrocers and Nick had watched his mother pick out some apples to buy. Near the apples and just at the right height for him to reach was an enormous basket of mixed fruits.

'Can we buy some of these too?' he asked, and stretched out his hand.

His mum pulled him away quickly and he almost fell over.

'Nicholas, please don't be naughty, can't you see the notice?'

Nick was puzzled.

'Look,' she said and pointed towards some writing. 'It says, "DO NOT TOUCH".'

'But Mum, I . . .'

She wasn't listening any more and they were quickly outside on the pavement again.

Nick hated shopping, especially when his mum was in a hurry.

'We must buy a birthday present for Gran,' she said and took Nick into a china shop.

After the busy street it was very quiet.

'You can help me choose something,' she said.

Nick knew she'd forgotten about the fruit, and decided he'd try to be good. He didn't want to be called Naughty Nick again.

The carpet on the shop floor was so thick you couldn't even hear your footsteps. Nick wondered why his mother whispered when she asked, 'Do you think Gran would like one of those little glass swans?'

He looked at them, swimming on a small glass-topped table. Thinking he would like to touch the beautiful swans, he moved forward and stretched out his hand.

'Nicholas,' said his mother and pulled him back to her side. 'The sign says "DO NOT TOUCH".'

'But Mum, I can't . . .'

She wasn't listening again.

'Come on, we'll go home. You're very naughty today.' And she walked quite fast, all the way home. Even though she held his hand, it was difficult to keep up with her. When they arrived Nick sat down and cried.

'I don't want to be called Naughty Nick . . . and, Mum, I can't *read*.'

This time she did listen. First she thought a bit and then said. 'I'm sorry, Nick, that was stupid of me. Dry your eyes – we'll both have a drink.'

'Are you still cross with me?'

'Not any more.' she said, and smiled.

Later, when Nick went into the lounge, he found his mum writing something.

'This is for you,' she said. 'I've made a sign, like the ones we saw today,' and she pointed out the words.

'This is DO, this is NOT, and this is TOUCH – DO NOT TOUCH.'

They repeated the words over again together.

'Can it be my sign?' Nick asked.

'Of course,' his mum replied.

Nick had great fun for the rest of the day – putting the sign beside some of his favourite toys.

A few days later when they went to the library,

there was a special display of models. Nick and his mum were looking at them when his friend Lucy and her mother came up to them.

Lucy put out her hand to touch one of the models.

'Don't touch, Lucy,' said Nick. 'That notice says "DO NOT TOUCH".' And he pointed out the words.

Lucy was amazed and told her mum, 'Nick can read.'

This made Nick feel proud and although he couldn't read books yet, he would always be able to read 'DO NOT TOUCH'.

Ten Big Giants

This is an action song or party game sung to the tune of 'Ten green bottles'. All the children are standing big and tall. They can either be marching on the spot or marching around as they sing.

Ten big giants, marching straight and tall.
Ten big giants, marching straight and tall.
One big giant did accidentally fall.
One falls down.
Nine big giants, standing straight and tall.

Nine big giants, marching straight and tall.
Nine big giants, marching straight and tall.
One big giant did accidentally fall.
Another falls down.
Eight big giants standing straight and tall.

Continue until no giants are left!

What Shall We Do?

One – two – what shall we do?
    Standing.
Three – four – sit on the floor.
    Sit on the floor.
Five – six – pretend to mix.
    Pretend you have a bowl and mix it up.
Seven – eight – I stayed up late.
    Yawn.
Nine – ten – start again!
    Jump up.

This time do it faster
        – and faster
                – and faster until you stop!

Sounds Like . . .

I'm thinking of a word
That sounds like *path*.
I'm wet all over when
I have a . . . .

I'm thinking of a word
That sounds like *tar*.
When I go for a ride
I sit in the . . . .

I'm thinking of a word
That sounds like *do*.
It isn't me – but it
Could be . . . .

I'm thinking of a word
That sounds like *chair*.
At the top of my head
Grows my . . . .

I'm thinking of a word
That sounds like *cat*.
It lies on the floor
And is called a . . . .

Things to Eat and Drink

a is for an alphabet of things to eat and drink.
b is for biscuits and blancmange coloured pink.

c is for coffee, chocolate cake and cheese.
d is for doughnuts that ooze when we squeeze.

e is for eggs, boiled, poached or fried.
f is for figs wrinkled and dried.

g is for gooseberries and grapefruit too.
h is for honey on bread that is new.

i is for ice-cream and icing on the cake.
j is for jelly and juicy jam to make.

k is for kipper – a very boney fish.
l is for loaf, and liver on a dish.

m is for milk and mustard and meat.
n is for nutmeg and nice nuts to eat.

o is for onion and juicy orange squash.
p is for potatoes, chips, boiled or mash.

q is for queen cakes with currants on top.
r is for rice pudding served nice and hot.

s is for spaghetti and sugar and sauce.
t is for tea – we drink it of course.

u is for ugli fruit, like a tangerine.
v is for vanilla, in an ice-cream.

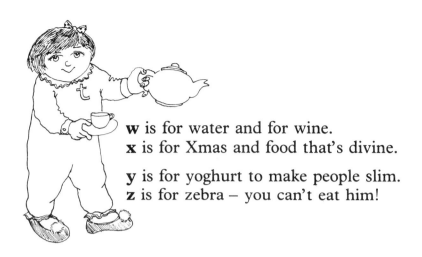

w is for water and for wine.
x is for Xmas and food that's divine.

y is for yoghurt to make people slim.
z is for zebra – you can't eat him!

Number One

All on its own is number *one*.
> *Hold up one finger and do the same every time*
> *'one' is mentioned.*
Only *one* moon and only *one* sun.
In every year there's only *one* May.
And only *one* morning in every day.
I've only *one* mouth and nose, you see.
> *Point to mouth and nose.*
There's only *one* you and only *one* me.
> *Point.*

Town Day

Trumper's Trip to Town

Trumper is an elephant – not an ordinary elephant by any means. He lives in a house, just like you and me, and he does all the things that you like doing.

He arrived in this country, a cold, wet, frightened little elephant, and was spotted by a lady who felt sorry for him.

'I'll have him if no one else wants him,' she said.

No one did. So she took him home, made him some warm socks, mitts, a jumper and a pair of check dungarees, and now he lives with the family. He even calls her Mum.

Trumper has a lot of things to learn. He is not used to traffic because there are no cars and lorries in the jungle, so he has to be particularly careful when he goes out.

He loves shopping. On one extra special day he was going on a shopping trip with his mum. He had saved enough money to buy a football. He was so excited and eager to start he opened the gate and ran down the pavement.

'Trumper, Trumper,' called his mum, but he took no notice.

Luckily elephants can't run very fast and his mum soon caught him, but she was *very annoyed*.

'How many times have I told you, never to go outside the gate unless I am with you?'

Trumper was sorry because he'd made a mistake and was determined to show what a clever elephant he could be. He walked along, holding his mum's hand, on the inside of the pavement, as good as gold.

When they came to the crossing in the town, he stopped first.

'That's very good,' said his mum. She was quite surprised to know that he remembered to *stop* and *look* – even at a crossing.

They waited until the traffic stopped, walked on to the black and white stripes and crossed safely. When they reached the other side Trumper looked up at the lights and winked back, as if to say, 'Thank you for being there.'

The first stop was at the bakers. Now elephants love jam buns and doughnuts and Trumper almost forgot about behaving himself. His trunk wriggled towards a tray full of buns and doughnuts – just as his mum turned to look at him.

That naughty baby elephant pretended he was waving to someone in the street!

Next was the toy shop and Trumper chose a beautiful black and white football. He wanted to carry it himself, but his mum said it would be safer in her bag.

They were going home by bus and as they waited at the bus stop, a big red double decker came into view. When it stopped, Trumper's mum lifted him up the steps and found a seat downstairs.

They had only travelled a short distance when Trumper whispered, 'Where's the seat belts?'

'You don't have seat belts in buses – only cars,' his mum answered.

The journey was soon over and Trumper was in a hurry to get off, so that he could play with his new football – his lovely black and white football.

'Wait until the bus has stopped,' said his mum.

She lifted him off and they waited on the pavement until it was out of sight. Trumper's mum was talking to a friend and he was looking at his football again, wishing she would hurry up.

His trunk wriggled towards it, touched it and moved it around. It was a super football. He wriggled it a little more and it fell out of the bag and rolled into the road – with Trumper after it.

His mum caught hold of his jumper and pulled

him back – just in time. There was a screech of brakes and then a bang!

Trumper's new football had been run over by a car and had burst!

'Just look at your football,' said his mum. 'If I hadn't caught hold of your jumper – *you* would have been squashed like that.'

Trumper was very frightened. He looked at the traffic and then at the squashed ball and held his mum's hand tightly until they reached home.

Trumper's trip to town and his narrow escape had made him tired. He fell fast asleep – wondering how long it would take him to save up for another football!

Crossing the Street

This is a traffic action rhyme for a group of children to act out. Some can be cars and lorries, and others people wanting to cross the street. Two could be Belisha Beacons, and one a lollipop person.

Lots and lots of motor cars, up and down the road,
Just as many lorries carrying a heavy load,
Listen to their hooters – peep – peep – peep.
Look, here come some children who want to cross
the street.

They look at all the traffic, travelling up and down.
Now, what should they do, to cross a road in town?
Yes – look for a crossing – it has a sign that's
bright,
And stripes across the road, painted black and
white.

The children see the crossing and stand at the kerb.
The cars and lorries stop – no hooters can be
heard.
As safe as safe can be, they walk across the street.
The cars and lorries start again – peep – peep –
peep.

I Spy

I see someone early in the day,
Riding on a bike or walking on his way.
Delivering a letter
   or maybe something better.
I am a . . . . . he will say.

Answer: Postman

I see someone every school day,
Stopping the traffic we meet on the way.
Standing up straight
   For us she will wait.
I am a . . . . . she will say.

Answer: Lollipop lady

Shiny and red, making a noise,
Out of its way go all the girls and boys.
Pipes and hoses and ladders on the top.
Oo-oo, Oo-oo and then stop.
Off jump the men, unwind the hose.
Stand back, please, mind your toes!

Answer: Fire engine

On buses, lorries, cars and bikes,
Vans and prams and little trikes,
Different sizes can be found
But the shape is always round.
Answer: Wheels

Make a
Bookworm Bookmark

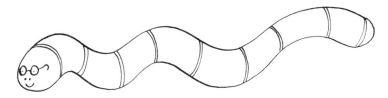

In the town you will find the library. If you choose
a book, you will need something to mark your page
with – so make yourself a bookworm bookmark.

What you need

A postcard or piece of card
Felt tips
Scissors

What you do

1   Trace the bookworm on to it (or draw your
    own shape).
2   Colour it.
3   Cut it out and it is ready to use.

Here is a rhyme about your bookworm.

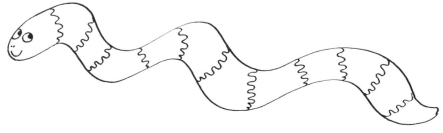

I'm a little bookworm, living in a book.
Turn the pages slowly, not too far to look.
I will always tell you where you stopped last time.
If you say 'How are you?' I'll say 'I am fine.'
Living in a book you'd think wouldn't be much
    fun,
Because I seem to be alone and never meet
    anyone.
But I'll tell you a secret – I'll share it just with
    you.
I meet the people in the book. Oh yes! It's really
    true.
They come alive and talk to me, on every single
    page.
It's lovely being a bookworm – no matter what
    your age!

Emma Goes Shopping

*Make the appropriate noises wherever you see
dashes like this ——.*

Emma held her mother's hand tightly, as they
walked along the pavement. There was so much
noise in the town: buses —— lorries —— cars with
horns —— and bicycles with bells ——.

They came to a crossing and still the traffic was
going fast ——. They pressed a button and waited
for the little red man to change to green. Emma
listened for the bleeping —— and they crossed
safely.

They passed a pram and the baby inside was

crying —— it didn't like the noise of the car horn
—— or the bicycle bell ——.

Emma asked her mother if she could stop at the
pet shop to look at the kittens —— birds —— and
puppies ——. They didn't have time that day,
there was so much shopping to do.

Inside the supermarket music was playing ——
and people were talking ——. Emma was pleased
when they had finished. Back out on the street
again the traffic was still busy —— as they waited
at the crossing. The red man changed to green and
bleeped —— the traffic stopped and Emma and
her mum were on their way home.

Home Day

Gran's New Home

Amy was feeling important. 'It's all right, you can leave me here,' she said to her big brother. 'It was ME she wanted to see.'

He waited until Gran opened the door and rode off on his bike.

'Hello, Gran,' said Amy. 'I've come to see your new house.'

Gran smiled. 'I wanted you to be my very first visitor.'

Amy walked inside. It didn't smell like Gran's house – it smelt like her bedroom after it had been painted. The room seemed light and instead of Gran's tiny windows with lots of plants there was only one big one.

'Where are your plants?'

'Plants like special windows. I've left them where they were happy.'

'Where's the picture of Dad and Aunty Grace when they were little? And where's Grandad's rocking chair?'

'They said there was only room for one chair in here. The other one is in the bedroom, come and see.'

Amy had a feeling she wasn't going to like Gran's new home.

'You've only got a little bed, like me.'

'That's all I need,' replied Gran.

Amy sat in the rocking chair, curled up her legs and started to rock.

'It's not right here. It needs to be facing yours.'

'That's just what I thought,' Gran answered, and between them they pushed and pulled until the chair was in the living room.

Soon they were facing each other again. Gran sat in her chair and Amy jumped into Grandad's and started rocking. It still didn't feel right. Then she remembered the picture and went to find it.

While she was in the bedroom she spotted the rug made of rags that used to be between the chairs. She rolled it up and dragged it along.

Gran had her eyes closed, so Amy put the old rug on top of the new one and placed the picture on the sideboard. She settled herself in the chair. She was glad Gran still had the clock because she liked to rock to and fro with the sounds.

'Tick – tock – tick – tock,' to and fro, to and fro and she could see the picture one way and the rug the other.

Gran opened her eyes and noticed the rug and the picture.

'What a clever girl you are, Amy. Let's have some tea.'

'Where's your old kettle?'

'Well that's one thing I didn't mind getting rid of,' she said. 'It took such a long time to boil. Just look at my lovely new electric one.'

'It's just like ours,' Amy said. 'Where's your old one gone?'

'It was an antique,' she replied. 'They paid me a lot of money for it.'

'What's anti . . . anti . . .?'

'Antique – means old and precious. There, look, the new one's boiling already.'

Amy was happy to see she still had her special mug, the one Dad used to use.

After tea they sat in the chairs again and Amy said, 'Gran, I do like your new home.'

Gran smiled. 'Yes, I'm liking it better now too.'

Amy was still thinking about the kettle and said, 'Gran – I hope they don't sell you.'

'Sell me?'

'Yes, well you're old and precious, so you must be an antique too!'

Amy could never understand why sometimes Gran seemed to laugh and cry at the same time. All she knew was that she loved her very much.

Katy Kitten

I am Katy Kitten with a coat of fur,
Stroke hands on body.
If you stroke me gently, you can hear me purr.
Make purring noise.
I have two eyes and two ears too,
Indicate eyes and ears.
A nose and a mouth – just like you.
Indicate and point.
I've a long wavy tail and four little feet.
Indicate as before.
I put out my tongue to drink and eat!
Put out tongue and wriggle it.
I'm always warm in my coat of fur.
Stroke hands on body.
Now listen quietly and hear me purr.
Purr – purr – purr.

In My House

I spy – something on the floor,
All around the room and underneath the door.
Quiet to walk on, soft to sit,
Snug and warm and cosy – a perfect fit.

Answer: Carpet

I spy – something I can eat,
It's white or brown and makes things sweet.
Put a spoonful in your tea.
You will be as sweet as me!

Answer: Sugar

I spy – somewhere I can sit.
No matter what your size, it will fit.
Used beside the table and to watch TV.
It usually has four legs – look and see.

Answer: Chair

My House

Make a house and the people who live inside it.

What you need

Plain paper
Felt tips, paints or crayons
Glue
Scissors

What you do

1   Cut out a piece of paper (about 30 cm × 15 cm) and fold it in half to make a square.
2   Draw a door at the centre of the folded edge and a roof shape at the top.
3   Cutting through both sides of the paper, cut out the door shape, and trim away the top to leave the roof shape.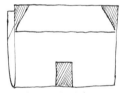

cut out shaded areas

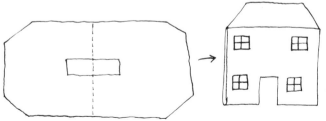

open out and put glue on roof area   then stick the two sides together

4   Open out and spread glue on the top part of your house, leaving the part round the door unglued, as shown in the picture.
5   Stick the two sides together.
6   Draw in the windows.
7   Colour and decorate your house.

Make the people and your door

1   Cut another strip of paper 25 cm long and the depth of your door.
2   In the centre of your strip draw a door to fit your house, and one or two people on either side.
3   Decorate the strip.

4   Thread the strip through the bottom of your house, until the door is in place. See who lives in the house by pulling the strips – first one way and then the other

81

1 Use photographs or small cut-out pictures of
   people and pets for the occupants.
2 Colour both sides of the house and strip, so
   that you have extra people living inside.
3 Instead of colouring the house, you could use
   sticky-back coloured paper for the windows and
   the roof.

Mrs Cat's Cake

Mrs Cat made a cake
  Of milk and bread.
'You should have used bones,'
  Mr Dog said.
'Oh no,' said the mouse.
  'Always use cheese.'
'Use worms,' said the bird.
  'Then I will be pleased.'
'Nuts,' said the squirrel.
  'Grass,' said the cow.
Mrs Cat replied,
  'In a cake? But how?
You make your own cake,
  I will make mine.
I like it this way –
  It tastes just fine.'

What Shall I Wear Today?

On wet days I wear wellingtons,
  To squish and squash about.
I always wear my sandals
  When the sun comes out.
My ordinary shoes I wear,
  Walking in the town.
But my slippers always peep
  From beneath my dressing gown!

Look Around

When you walk into a ~~room~~, take a look around.
Use your eyes to *see* if dangers can be found.
Is a guard around the fire? Are the rugs all neat?
Even toys left on the floor get in the way of feet.
If our feet get tangled up, we bump down on the
  ground.
So when you walk into a ~~room~~, take a look
  around.

Early in the Morning

Early in the morning
  When I am in my bed,
I listen to the noises
  That come into my head.
I hear the bottles rattling
  As the milkman makes his call.
I hear the postman at the door,
  And there's a letter in the hall.
The paperboy is whistling
  Such a happy song,
And then I hear the big red bus
  Rumbling along.
I stretch and then I wriggle
  Before I'm out of bed.
I like the morning noises
  I hear inside my head.
But my favourite of them all,
  It makes me feel just fine,
Is when I hear the call,
  'Come on – it's breakfast time!'

84

Seaside Day

Roy the Hat Boy
Goes to the Seaside

Note to storyteller: The rhyme about Roy and his hat is repeated several times, and it is fun for the children/child to join in each time it is repeated.

Roy had been looking forward to his day at the seaside for a long time. At last it was here and he was helping his mum and dad unload the boot of the car.

Roy is the boy who loves wearing hats and whenever his friends see him they say, 'Here comes Roy – and his hat' and when they see which hat he's wearing they say, 'Well I never – fancy that!'

Today Roy was wearing a straw sun hat.

'Here you are, Roy, you can carry your bucket and spade and flags for your sandcastle,' said Dad.

Mum carried the picnic basket, Dad carried the chairs and they walked towards the beach. On the way they met a family they knew and of course they said,

'Here comes Roy – and his hat.

Well I never – fancy that!'

His friend Anna was wearing a sun hat, just like Roy's.

This made them both laugh and they all continued towards the beach. It was difficult to find a spare place. It looked as if everyone else had decided to visit the seaside today.

'Here we are,' said Dad. 'I think this spot is big enough for us,' and he dropped the chairs on the hot sand.

Whilst the grown ups were getting settled Roy and Anna looked around at all the people.

'What a lot of people,' said Anna. 'And what a lot of hats.'

Roy couldn't ever remember seeing so many people wearing hats. He was sure no one here would say,

'Here comes Roy – and his hat.

Well I never – fancy that!'

'Look,' said Anna. 'There's someone else with a hat like ours . . . and another . . . and another. Roy, there's lots of hats just like ours.'

'Come here a minute, you two,' said Dad, and he explained to them how important it was not to wander away. 'You'll never find us in this crowd and we'd have great difficulty finding you.'

Anna's dad said, 'I've an idea, give me your hats a moment.' And on the band around Roy's hat, he wrote 'Roy North' in big letters and then his address in smaller letters. He did the same on Anna's hatband.

'Now our hats are different from all the others,' said Anna.

'Mine's still the same as yours though,' said Roy.

'No, it isn't,' replied Anna. 'My name and address are different from yours.'

But Roy still felt that no one would say,

'Here comes Roy – and his hat.

Well I never – fancy that!'

'Do you want to have a paddle in the sea?' asked the two dads.

'Yes, please,' yelled Anna and Roy, and they rushed to take off their shoes and socks.

They walked in and out and around the people until they reached the water.

'Ow,' shouted Roy. 'It's very cold.'

'Yes it is,' replied Anna. 'I don't like it. It's *too* cold.'

'All right, we'll come back later,' said her dad. 'Let's have our picnic first.'

Walking back, Roy was pleased he had hold of his dad's hand. He couldn't see his mum anywhere. Everyone looked the same.

'Where's Mum?' he asked.

'Here I am,' she answered, and Roy felt pleased to see her.

He knew then he didn't want to move very far away, and decided to make sandcastles.

'Can I have one of your flags for the top of my sandcastle?' asked Anna.

'Just one,' said Roy, because he had an idea.

He took off his hat and pushed the other flags all around behind the hatband. Now his hat was different – no one else was wearing one with flags.

'That's a good idea,' said Dad. 'Now we'll be able to see exactly where you are.'

But that wasn't the reason he'd done it. He just wanted his hat to be different so that everyone would say,

'Here comes Roy – and his hat.
Well I never – fancy that!'

Pretend

Let's pretend we're at the seaside,
Sitting on the sand.
> *Sit on floor or chair.*

The sun is shining brightly.
> *Look upwards.*

We've got ice-creams in our hands.
> *Pretend to hold an ice-cream.*

Take a lick – it's cold as ice.
> *Pretend to lick.*

Take another. Oh, that's nice.
> *Continue licking.*

It's melting now – so finish it fast,
> *Quickly eat it up.*

And watch the people going past.
> *Sit back and relax, moving head to and fro.*

88

Make an Octopus

What you need

A ball (ping pong/polystyrene/rubber/cotton, etc.)
Sequins (for eyes)
Felt (for nose and mouth)
Ribbon, wool or 4 pipe-cleaners (orange/pink or
    grey)
Old pencil or empty pen tube or length of dowel
Glue

What you do

1   Glue ball to pencil/pen tube/dowel (paint it
    first if necessary).
2   Cut out two noses from felt. One happy
    mouth, one sad.
3   Glue into position to make a face on either side
    of ball. Add sequins for eyes.
4   Cut out eight legs from ribbon, wool or pipe-
    cleaners (half a pipe-cleaner for each leg). If
    you are using wool or ribbon, to make it curl
    rub it over with glue and roll up until dry.
5   Glue the legs into place around the ball. You
    have an octopus who can be happy or sad!

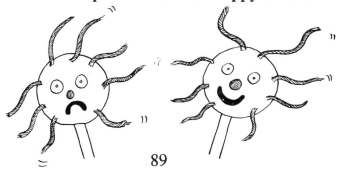

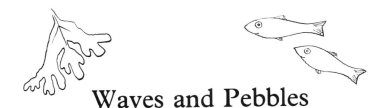

Waves and Pebbles

Listen to the waves on the sea's shore,
    Splishing and splashing for evermore.
Coming in and going out,
    Splishing, splashing all about.

Pebbles

Pebbles on the beach, large and small,
    Rough and humpy bumpy, or round like a ball.
Standing on a big one, with wings all spread.
    Is a black-headed gull, waiting for some bread.
Give him some and what will he do?
    Flap his wings and squawk 'Thank you.'

David's Pebble

When David went to the seaside
  He brought a pebble home.
His friends all said to him,
  'It's just a silly stone.'
'I like it,' David said,
  'Because it's smooth and round.
You'll never see a stone like this
  Lying on the ground.
I'm going to make it into something,
  Just you wait and see.'
Then he found his felt tip pens
  And drew, quite full of glee.
He drew some eyes, a nose and mouth,
  It really did look great.
It wasn't a pebble any more –
  But David's new playmate!

The a, b and sea

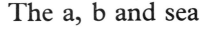

a is for all things found near the sea.
b is the beach where we play happily.
c is for caves and the cliffs so high.
d is for donkeys as they trot by.
e is for eel, the fish like a snake.
f is for fishermen, whose bait it will take.
g is for gulls flying up around.
h is a sea-horse that sometimes is found.
i is for ice-cream we all love to eat.
j is for jellyfish – not very sweet!
k is for kite, near the sea it flies well.
l is for limpets that live in a shell.
m is for mackerel all silvery grey.
n is the net to catch one today.
o is for oysters that sometimes grow pearls.
p is the pier – full of boys and girls.
q is for quiet to listen to the waves.
r is for rocks at the entrance to caves.
s is for seaweed, for shells and for sand.
t is for tide when it comes towards land.
u is for umbrella to block out the sun.
v is for voyage – on the sea it is fun.
w is for water that makes us all wet.
x is for something I can't think of yet!
y is for yacht sailing on the blue sea,
zig-zag it goes, carrying you and me.

Easter Days

The Moonstruck Chicken

In the farmyard a fluffy yellow chicken flapped his tiny wings and cheeped. 'I'm *not* an Easter chick. I *do not* want to be an Easter chick. I AM A MOON CHICKEN!'

'We are Easter chicks, so you must be one too,' replied his brothers and sisters.

'I am *not*,' he said.

Mother Hen explained to him. 'You were born at Easter time, so you must be an Easter chick.'

'I AM A MOON CHICKEN,' he cheeped again as loudly as possible.

'Chickens cannot live on the moon,' they told him.

'I can,' he said.

'Don't be a silly chicken. You're no different from us.'

'One day, when my wings have grown, I will fly back there,' he announced.

Mother Hen realized that he really believed he was a Moon Chicken. She decided to take the other chicks to look for worms and leave him dreaming about his journey to the moon.

As she pecked about the ground she wondered what could be done to stop him being so silly.

Just then, the wind blew something over the farmyard wall. She looked up and there, gently floating down towards them, was a large yellow balloon.

'Is it the moon come to fetch our brother?' they asked.

'No, of course not. It's only a yellow balloon,' Mother Hen told them. 'But I have an idea. Come, help me catch it, please.'

The wind made the balloon float up and down. At last Mother Hen held the string in her beak and tied it to a large stone.

Then she called. 'Moon chicken, Moon chicken.'

The chick was delighted that at last his mother knew he was a Moon Chicken. When he was near enough to see the yellow balloon, he stopped.

'What's that?' he asked.

'It's the moon,' replied his mother. 'If you are a Moon Chicken, you should know that.'

'Yes, I did – really,' he answered slowly.

'Jump on it then,' said his Mother. 'I expect it's come to fetch you. Now you will not have to wait for your wings to grow.'

He looked at the balloon. He walked around it. He looked at it again. Then, with his tiny beak – he pecked it.

POP! went the balloon – and the chick was SO frightened.

'I don't want to be a Moon Chicken,' he cried. 'Please can I be an Easter chick?'

'Of course you can,' replied Mother Hen, and she smiled to herself.

Church Bells

Listen, listen, to the church bell.
Hand behind ear.
What do you think it's trying to tell?
Point finger.

Ding dong, ding dong, very loud,
Pretend to pull bells.
Ding dong, ding dong, telling the crowd,
Pretend to pull bells.
'Come inside and look around.'
Beckon towards yourself.
Listen to my loud, loud sound.
Hand behind ear again.

Ding dong, ding dong, ding dong,
Pull bells.
Goes my long, long, ding dong song.

What Am I?

Sometimes I am white,
  Sometimes I am brown.
Buy me in the country,
  Buy me in the town.
I'm a roundish shape
  With a soft inside.
And your breakfast, dinner or tea,
  I can provide.
Tap me gently,
  Then I break my shell.
Eat me up –
  And say 'Farewell.'

Answer: Egg

Sometimes I am dark brown,
  Sometimes pale.
Always at Eastertime
  I am on sale.
I'm nice to eat,
  Or so they say.
You can open me up
  On Easter Day.
I've a shiny coat,
  I'm packed in a box.
Sometimes I'm filled right up
  with chocs!

Answer: Chocolate egg

Make an Easter Basket

What you need

Polystyrene egg cartons
Pipe-cleaners
Coloured cotton wool balls
Scissors

What you do

1 Cut out the egg shapes into pairs.
2 Make two holes in the centre join.
3 Push pipe-cleaner through and bend it flat
   underneath to secure handle.
4 Pat a small amount of cotton wool in each side.

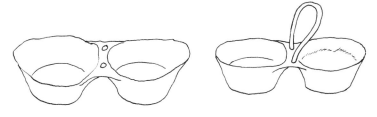

Ideas for filling the basket

A few tiny Easter eggs in each side.
A small fluffy chick in one side and eggs in the
   other.
Any small toy or animal.
Flowers (real or artificial).

Make an Easter Tree

What you need

Coloured egg cartons
A very 'twiggy' small branch
Cotton
Glue
Oddments of lace or ribbon
Flower pot (or something similar) filled with earth
  or sand

What you do

1 'Plant' your branch in a pot of earth or sand.
   To make it secure finish off with about 2 cm
   Polyfilla.

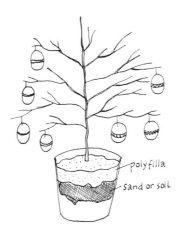

2 Cut out the egg shapes of the
   cartons.

3 Tie a knot in one end of a piece of cotton and thread through the centre of egg shape.

4 Glue around edge of egg shape and stick another shape to it. Glue a piece of lace or ribbon around the 'join'. Hang on your tree.

glue together

5 Make as many as you like and experiment with other decorations, e.g. sequins, beads, etc.

6 *Extra idea* – put a small present inside each egg.

Make an
Eggshell Humpty

Note: Either use a small piece of card for individual Humpties or a large piece for a group one.

What you need

Eggshells
Sheet of card or postcard
Glue
Felt tip pens

What you do

1 Break or crunch the eggshells.
2 Draw an egg shape outline on the card. Draw in eyes and nose and mouth.
3 Spread glue all over egg shape (except eyes, etc.). Press the eggshells on top.
4 Draw in arms, legs and a hat and you have a Humpty for yourself.

Christmas Days

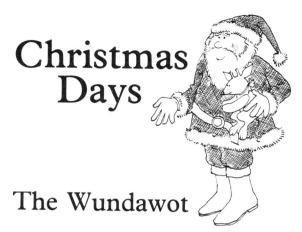

The Wundawot

Mr Snooze helped in Father Christmas's toy factory. He must have been at least two hundred years old, but he couldn't remember. In fact Mr Snooze couldn't remember anything.

When Father Christmas found him, he had even forgotten his name.

'I'll have a little snooze,' he said. 'Maybe when I wake up, I'll remember.' He often had a little snooze – but he never did remember, anything.

'I shall call you Mr Snooze,' announced Father Christmas. 'You can stay here and help me in my toy factory.'

He was delighted and all went well – until Christmas. It was such a busy year that all Father Christmas's helpers had to help him deliver. If Mr Snooze went with them he would never remember his way home – so he was left behind, in charge of the toy factory.

Father Christmas collected every toy he could find, they all waved goodbye and off they went.

It was rather quiet and lonely for Mr Snooze when they had gone, so he decided to start making some more toys. He looked around for one to copy but there was nothing left, and, of course, he couldn't remember what anything looked like.

'Oh well,' he said to himself. 'I'll make some fluffy animals. I think I might be able to remember which pieces fit together.'

He found material, bodies, legs, tails, ears, eyes and noses, and started sewing them together. He continued until he had filled two shelves with animals – then he fell fast asleep!

When Father Christmas returned, he went into the workshop to see if he could find just a few more toys for last minute orders. What a surprise he had when he looked at the shelves.

He was happy to see some toys there, but whatever were they supposed to be? He picked one up and said, 'I wonder what *this* is?'

It seemed to have a bear's body, a rabbit's feet, a giraffe's head and a long tail. Just as he was trying to puzzle it out, two helpers walked in.

'I wonder what *this* is?' said one.

'Old Mr Snooze must have made it,' replied the other. 'We didn't leave him anything to copy and he couldn't remember how the pieces fitted together.'

Just then Mr Snooze himself came in and saw them holding his animals.

'Mr Snooze, whatever have you done,' asked Father Christmas. 'This isn't like anything I know.'

'I wonder what it is?' mumbled Mr Snooze and as he said it, he shouted, 'That's it – it's a WUNDAWOT!'

Father Christmas wasn't particularly pleased, but time was short. So he put them in his sack and rushed off.

Old Mr Snooze was still trying to remember what they were, when Father Christmas arrived back again.

'Mr Snooze, you're a genius,' he shouted. 'Everyone loves your Wundawots, we must make lots more, for next year.'

This made Mr Snooze very happy and off he went mumbling, 'I hope I can remember how to make some more Wundawots!'

Have you ever seen a WUNDAWOT. See if you can draw one!

Father Christmas

The storyteller reads the story and pauses where indicated . . . for the children/child to make the sounds. For example, when the word is 'cold' . . . you say: 'Brrrrr'. When the word is 'windy' . . . you say: 'Oooo-oooo'. When the word is 'shivered' . . . you chatter your teeth. And every time Father Christmas is mentioned you call out, 'Jingle bells, jingle bells'.

It can be really funny if you record your performance on cassette or tape recorder. You'll be surprised at the results.

It was Christmas Eve and the night was cold . . . and windy . . . Father Christmas . . . was ready to leave. He patted his cat . . . and dog . . . and went outside. He shivered . . . and the cold . . . made him sneeze.

He found his sleigh and shot off like a rocket . . . On and on he went, over towns . . . country . . . and sea . . . . When he heard some carol singers . . . he knew it was time to stop and pulled hard on the reins.

Father Christmas . . . walked . . . across the rooftop, hoping all the children were fast asleep . . . . He climbed into a chimney and let out a yell . . . . It was rather small for him, but he wriggled about and eventually landed with a plop . . . on the hearth.

104

Father Christmas . . . looked around and decided to leave a drum . . . a whistle . . . and a book about Tarzan . . . . He saw that something had been left for him, so he ate the biscuit . . . and had a drink . . . before he left through the door . . . .

He soon finished all his work, but it was still cold . . . and windy . . . and now it was starting to snow . . . . At last he reached home and he was soon in bed and fast asleep . . . .

When he woke on Christmas Day it was indeed a white Christmas . . . and his cat . . . and dog . . . joined with him to sing 'Jingle Bells' . . . .

Make Some
Christmas Bells

What you need

Silver foil
Egg carton
White cotton
Scissors
One wire coat hanger (if you want to make a
  mobile)

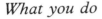

What you do

1 Cut out the egg shapes and cover with foil.
2 Cut different lengths of cotton for each bell.
3 Tie a knot and thread it through the top. The
   bell is ready to hang on your tree.

For a bell mobile

1 Make five or six bells.
2 Cover the coat hanger with silver foil by
   winding strips of it round and round.

3 Hang bells from it.
4 Tie a strong piece of thread to the handle and hang it up. Watch your mobile move with every wisp of air.

Baby Jesus

At Christmas time a baby came,
  Baby Jesus was his name.
His mother rocked him on her arm,
  Protecting him from every harm.
She rocked him gently to and fro
  And many came to say 'Hello'.
In the stable on a bed of hay
  Jesus was born on Christmas Day.

Make Santa in a Chimney

What you need

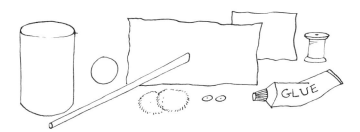

A square/oblong or round carton (about 10 cm
   high)
Piece of dowel 20 cm long
2 pieces of red material. One to fit around con-
   tainer 10 cm high. One 6 cm square.
Ping pong or polystyrene ball
Cotton wool
Felt or sequins or beads or buttons for eyes
Wallpaper in brick or stone design
Glue

What you do

1   Glue the ball on to your dowel.
2   Glue your larger piece of material
     together along the 10 cm side,
     as shown.
3   Gather one of the longer sides of
     this piece and glue it underneath
     the 'head'.

1

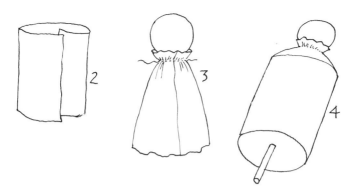

4   Make a hole in the bottom of
    your carton and guide the dowel
    through.
5   Glue the loose end of material
    around the top edge of carton.
6   Glue on cotton wool for beard
    and hair. Glue on eyes.

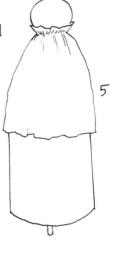

7   Cut the other piece of material
    into a triangle and glue the two
    short sides together to make a
    hat.

8 Glue the hat on to Father Christmas's head.

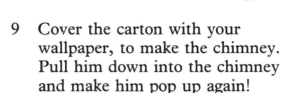

9 Cover the carton with your wallpaper, to make the chimney. Pull him down into the chimney and make him pop up again!

X is for Xmas

a is for apples and almonds to eat.
b is for balloons – a Christmas treat.
c is for crackers and the carols we hear.
d is for decorations that dangle everywhere.
e is for envelopes with cards inside.
f is Father Christmas who has a long ride.
g is for glitter – it shines day and night.

h is for holly with berries so bright.
i is for icing on the cake so fine.
j is for Jesus – born at this time.
k is for kings who brought gifts from afar.
l is the light – the shepherds saw a star.
m is for mistletoe hung above the door.
n is for nuts and nice things in store.
o is for oranges, juicy and sweet.
p is for postman and parcels so neat.
q is for queen – the fairy on the tree.
r is for robin, peeping in at you and me.
s is for snow falling soft and white.
t is for tree, such a pretty sight.
u is for umbrellas, the carol singers hold.
v is for their visit on a night that's cold.
w is for a wish for Happy Christmas days.
x is for Xmas – you can spell it both ways.
y is for you and your family too.
z is for zest in all that you do!